Live Poems Love Poems

Live Poems Love Poems
4x6 First Edition Paperback
978-0-9984381-2-2
Published by Secret Midnight Press

www.secretmidnightpress.com

LIVE POEMS
LOVE POEMS

by Ashley Dun and Jesse Cale

Illustrations by Chavilah Bennett
Layout by Jason Turner

LIVE

I caught myself in the mirror today
counting scars that I've collected
from scrapes and falls and brawls
and tallied times I've felt rejected

I kept the score of life's games
A mark for every time I lost
Becoming indebted to a darkness
Finding ways to pay the cost

But I noticed how they caught the light
My scars shown different from my skin
They reflected brighter than the rest
The way that hope does shine within

The greatest lesson that I learned
"To love myself is to forgive"
And even though I still know darkness
I'm glad I chose to live

—*Jesse Cale*

BEFORE SPRING

head splits
and aches and bleeds
and sorrow seeps out of
my pores despite
my posture
despite my smile
and my white teeth
my heart ebbs and flows
like the tide scraping rocks
and I feel it all
and you know all that I
know and it's okay
to hurt and to
cry and to crack
and the red spills out and
we stand and we smile and
we break and
it's going to be,
it has to be,
beautiful
in the end

—*Ashley Dun*

3

SPRING

I left my face there
On the ground by the pond
Lily pads and frogs and my face
Splashing onto my cheeks
from leaps

My lungs are a bindle of
green and spring

And my fists are blooming
buds as the sun hums

Spring is life's favorite song
And it plays like a yawn

The wind sails along my skin
And sinks in like a whisper

A feeling explained with a wiggle
And taught with a touch

My pace kneads a place for
lovely lush things

And the sun spins quarters
through the branches of trees

My voice is a puzzle
Each word is afloat

Like a chandelier of butterflies
Or notating a wind chime

I want a mouth like the sky
So I can swallow this moment

I want the arms of a mother
So I can hold it with love

I'd be a fisherman of time
Casting nets to catch seconds

And I'd sleep forever
If this was a dream

—*Jesse Cale*

WOUNDED

in those quiet
moments before
sleep
do you think of
me?
I swear I feel your skin
on mine and we're
swaying
in and out like
the tide
a warm whisper in
my ear and
suddenly you're
here wrapped
around me like a
bandage and it
couldn't be more
fitting

—*Ashley Dun*

EVERY WORD

I'm staring out the window as I write this
Sitting stories high

I turned off every light
My own little room of night

There are faint greys from outside
Casting darker shadows on my face

Every moment that I've counted
and every second that I've lost

Has brought me to this window
And everything to follow

Life put into words
can find the beauty in every scene

So find me writing and recounting
until there's nothing left unseen

—*Jesse Cale*

THE NIGHT, MY LOVE

Romance me, my slow dance partner
Not a being, but the night

I'm living for loving every secret that you keep
and how you play each star as light

and how you send everyone home
for me to safely roam alone
and you hold the breath of day in tight

If I'm to fall in love they'll have to be
As romantic as the night

—*Jesse Cale*

HEART'S HARBOR

Quickly climb closer and kiss me on the face
And twinkle little sparkles
And dash down the branches
To the stars in the sunlight
And my home in the mountains
We're salty babies
And nothing is old
You're my heart's harbor

—*Jesse Cale*

FROZEN

I'm thawed when
the heat of your breath
on my neck
brings me back to life
your whisper
stings my ear and I'm
suddenly a spark
my eyes alive
for you
devouring every piece
of you
and I burn until I'm
holy
ashes
all around

—Ashley Dun

DISTANCE

last night
I dreamt of you
it felt like cool
water flowing through
my caves and then
I woke up
hot and humbled
drowning in
daylight and the
distance between
my dream and
you feels like
galaxies like
land mine-filled
fields and
I can't decide
whether or not
it's worth the
journey

—*Ashley Dun*

MUSE

I love the musing of a brief romance
I drink up the emotion like a milkshake
I feel like a careless thief making noise inside the heart
I'll pull each loose thread like something's tied to the
other end
Like a song or a poem
Or a painting
Something else

So leave me a trail of sweets
I'll follow right along
I'm coming just to feel
Enough to write a song

Speak a word and let me listen
I'm bathing in our time
But I'll be going once
I've filled my stanza with our rhyme

And it hurts me too
To break my own heart
But love is everything
and I love art

—*Jesse Cale*

19

BALANCE

you are the shadows in
the moon that make me feel
small but beautiful
and you are the weeds in
the garden that
drive me crazy but still
remind me of summer and warmth
and I'll never get around you because
you are the clouds that block
the sunlight saving me from
the burn but also
bringing rain and
it's the balance
that keeps me sane

—*Ashley Dun*

52.

there's this
beating in my chest
that belonged to you
as the leaves were born on barren branches
your name bloomed within me and
created a home there
you were a cherry blossom
and I inhaled your scent like
a healing breath
I saw the sky alive in your eyes and felt
my heart like a hummingbird
and without warning
your petals wilted and fell around me
leaving me with a withered memory
a hope so temporary and every day
I see the tree you lived on that is now
flowerless but I know like spring
love will always return
it will heal this heart in pieces like petals
and the promise of cherry blossoms
makes me whole
as I call this
beating in my chest
my own

—*Ashley Dun, from Smoke Signals*

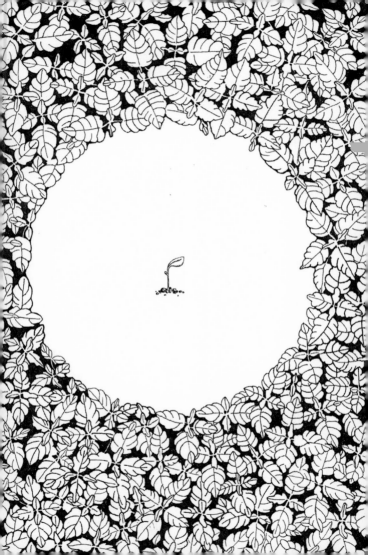

AN EMPTY SPACE

A moment's a harbor
between each, the sea
An empty space
Where loneliness will be

Where I breathe shadows
No sleep, no rest
An empty space
A hollow, in my chest

Where joy is misplaced
The narratives lull
An empty space
To continue at all

And I often forget
that I'm just passing through
An empty space
As we all sometimes do

—*Jesse Cale*

STAINED

they'll never know
the words
whispered in the
dark under the
summer moon and
they'll never know
the music
that plays when
I think of you
secrets weave
a tangled web
between us and
I can't quite seem
to get your scent
out of my
soul

—*Ashley Dun*

SUMMER'S DRESS

High above the sun she swam
Singing down the pour of the shine
She was sweet and golden
She was honey in the summer
Warm and sugar

From her mouth I see a flower
As the sun bursts behind her
She's as smooth and fragile as an eggshell
As she dances through my mind
In a field of wild flowers
She kisses me

—*Jesse Cale*

A BELL OR BALLERINA

Oh what she was
A portmanteau of destiny and fire
But a lifelong linguist can't say

She's the song of every bird I've heard
And the set of every sun I've seen
But just for now

Handmade and
She plays her body like an instrument conducted by God
The quiet notes of her expression are melodies in my eyes
Her presence, forte!

My heart climbs into my lungs
and out with every word I speak
And as if I'm to perform at any moment
Abashed by the scurry of my tongue
A blush to dress my face

I wait
To see
What I
Will be

To her
—*Jesse Cale*

31

STOLEN SENSES

it's been
one year but
god your scent still
sets my skin on fire
like dry grass in august and
god I need you
like the rain because
my fingers feel empty without yours and
the air seems too thin without your breath
so please just please
don't forget me because
god it hurts to feel
so little and
everything
all at once

—*Ashley Dun*

AU REVOIR!

My dear
Have fun
and be in love!
I'm waving handkerchiefs to you!
A little flag or tiny kite to wish you well
and my heart might say goodbye

You were a throb to each pain of my toes
but there was a sweet fragrance to each word you spoke

You tickled me each way I never wanted you to do
Oh if you were just someone else
How sad to be loved by the one we cast away
and how sweet to be loved in the way we've longed to be
loved

Cut deep into the sea now
May your bow find Neverland
or at least places peacefully paced for
however your feet make haste

—*Jesse Cale*

KNOW

you were born from the universe
close your eyes and see the galaxy
open them and watch the stardust dance
milky moons wash over you
moss makes up your insides and
you bleed lava
feel the burn of change on your flesh
groan with the ancient trees and
know, if only,
this:
your spirit is spectacular

—*Ashley Dun*

BUMBLEBIRD
AKA
FALLING ASLEEP VIII

Bumblebird
You're sweet to me
I'm sleepy now
Come speak to me
My eyes are faint
So see for me
Coming slowly down
Your bumble tree

—*Jesse Cale*

ARISE

the mattress beneath her
creaks under the pressure
she closes her eyes and cracks
each knuckle one by one
desperately trying to feel she
slows her breathing and
closes her eyes
lashes intertwine and
all is dark as the
silence screams
when will it end? or more accurately,
when will it begin?
her eyelids lift with her body
off of this old mattress in this old house
placing her feet on the ground her
soul demands:
arise

—*Ashley Dun*

MOON MILK

Drinking moon milk
and my eyes are closed!
Every pore is a mouth
and I'm lapping up life like I'm longing to glow

Singing each star
and the notes that they mean!
Everywhere's a song
and my lungs through my face into the sweet light of space!

Tying the wind
and the promise of a finger!
Each gust is a ribbon
and I'm garnished in moments from where they have been!

—*Jesse Cale*

HEAT

one day
two years
tight chest
weary eyes
time flies and
drags like a broken leg
aching and suffering
longing for freedom
breaking the chains of
time and space
crossing the border
of the universe
to float like a star
glowing like warm
coals in a raging fire

—*Ashley Dun*

KNOCK KNOCK, THE DOOR TO HELL

Quiver quiver bumble bee
A garden song that's sung to me

In a wistful air of aromas from before
Up memory's steps to emotion's door

Knock knock a type of tipping tow
Tip me to drown in the undertow

Each day of ours once remembered well
But to think of you now is the door to hell

—Jesse Cale

EVERYTHING

some days
i
don't exist
my body moves me
muscles bend and stretch
my lungs expand and
i
go on
trees and leaves and
people spin around me and
i
act and
i
breathe and
i
survive but
i
am not here
i
function and
i
forget that
i
am everything

—*Ashley Dun*

ONE WITH THE CLOUDS

melt into the earth
sea foam over rocks
swallow and exhale
feel free and one
with the clouds
feel your fingertips brush
the Galaxy
and tears bubbling over
volcanic explosion
of purpose
your heart beats with the
stampedes in the west
you are both mother and child
the Stars spell out your name
and you are
here
and you are
whole

—*Ashley Dun*

WE WANT TO LIVE THIS WAY

Corazón de la lune
Corazón de la lune
I'm looking to you
the heart of the moon

I'm spinning reflections
in a field of shadows
We're chasing our youth
down old paths of moments

Deep longing to live
To be seen having lived
To have lived a full life
And to be full of life

But dust like a minute
Settles somewhere unseen
Time has gone missing
And life was a dream

—*Jesse Cale*

FINITE

dark black
surrounds as I count down
the moments left of today
until tomorrow becomes today
and we continue holding our breath
until we're one with the sky
blue in the face won't get us
to the place we long for most
tomorrow does not exist
we only have a second to do
infinite things
to be everywhere and everyone
just hold on like roots in a storm
breathe life into your lungs
fresh release
march
forward
and be.

—*Ashley Dun*

TO TEASE AND TICKLE THE HEART

Words are a game
And to tempt love is laughter
Not in the deep parts of bellies
But in the shallows of each nerve

Teasing up a storm
Flirting with the undertow

Gambling with what weighs long to a spirit
And the ransom is always pieces of the heart

Thieving for a cure
Or just poaching desire
Whatever it may be
You're not a lover, but a liar

—*Jesse Cale*

WHEN YOU'RE CUTE

Cute is a bouncing piece of the sun
As cute as a button
As cute as a bird

Cute is a berry held tight in your palm
As cute as a wiggle
As cute as a noise

When your mouth curls up like a ribbon of pink
As cute as the morning
As sweet as a breeze

And from the moment I see you
Till the moment I sleep
As cute as the picture
Of you that I keep

—*Jesse Cale, from Mentha Spicata El Corazon!*

START

gold velvet on the skin
soft edges sinking in
and the dim lighting fills
your lungs and your soul
is full of Egyptian cotton
smooth silk seeps into your pores
and as the smoke raises to heaven
your fears dissolve and you are
one with the seafoam salty breeze
abandon anxiety and ditch depression
as you inhale deeply and hear
the crackling fire
singeing your sadness
burning your burdens to the ground
as each vessel brims boldly
with a bright elation you didn't
know existed glowing off of you.
every morning
is a new season
and you
are a new you.

—*Ashley Dun*

LUSTING FOR SPIDERS

I want your mind, words, and body
I want to twist them in a ballet of romance

Tie a knot with your neck to remind me of a master
Drown us both in an ink from the well of every word

Your darkness is a perfume that I'm drunk for through hallways
You linger like a taste or to my eyes a glim

Hollow every swallow left wanting just a bite
Shine has shown but in a daze as aimless as the night

—Jesse Cale

MUSIC

Some songs
strike a note
and just like that
I start to float

—Jesse Cale

SPARK

like tiny dust particles
reflecting in the morning light
our lives are a glimmer
in time
caught by the eye of the
universe for just an instant
a freckle in the eye of a
homeless man clinking change in a
bucket we are unnoticed and overall
unnecessary to the world spinning
around the sun more times
than you'll blink your eyes
and if that doesn't terrify you
nothing will

—Ashley Dun

HEART TO MEMORY

Too often talks of two tip toes
And no notes notating a noble nose
One whose prose pose the woes of a rose
The rush of a crush like a tart in the heart
But like sand through a hand
Or wind in a web
Love leaves, left alone
But memory makes my mind melt
And smiles stay and simmer somewhere sweet and
subtle

—*Jesse Cale*

NEW

making up for lost time
creating and recreating
shedding skin and
exhaling the dust of life
and rising with the sun
forget the darkness like a dream
cling with clenched fists
to the light

—*Ashley Dun*

DISTANCE

she unfolds like
pages in your favorite
book like
a purple rose in spring
and you ache for her
longing to discover
the rhythm in her breath
the pattern her eyelashes flutter as
she breathes in time with
the tide

—*Ashley Dun*

I LOVE YOU

It's hard to not
To say I love you to a stranger
A breeze on my back and my blue eyes
They can see
And your brown hair has no knots
Your dance, your hands,
To sing, and you do!
You do sing and you do it well.

Like spring water
A brook from my lungs
Words falling out the door
"I love you" I say in this moment
I'll use the word as if I never knew what love meant.

Certainly I do not love you
But from here
Up here
On my tip toes from enjoyment
From a burst of excitement and awe
Like a grunt from a blow
Out comes "I love you."

— *Jesse Cale, from Mentha Spicata El Corazon!*

SLOWLY

fingertips on skin like
soft whispers in candle light,
hot breath on a cold night and
we dance,
unsure of the steps but our
bodies blaze as we sway
in the moonlight,
hoping morning never comes

—Ashley Dun

MENTHA SPICATA EL CORAZON II

Always live your life with curious eyes
Unbridle your mind
Set a sail in your heart
And wiggle the toes of your soul

—Jesse Cale

3.

I am drenched in
life and dehydrated from
living
and I can't find
ground to stand on when
I see every life I'm not living
and I am constantly crushed
by the
monotony of the life I am
living and I can't even
breathe with this
toxic air of unhappiness
and fear and
each day is our last because
no one will ever know which
breath is our last
so I cry out for meaning
and I dig my fingernails
into the soil because
it's the only thing that's real
and
I'm not ready to let go of this
reality because it's all I know
and
I'm not ready to give in to

what I don't know so feet
don't fail me now
lets run until the horizon blurs
and the heat of the sun burns
and please
let me die by
the fire
of life

—*Ashley Dun,*
from Smoke Signals

TRYING

your velvet night
sky soul
slips through my
fingers, and
your moonbeam
madness is
always just out
of reach

—*Ashley Dun*

SWEET MIND, KEEP ME ALIVE

Today
To not
To choose
To live

Is larger to ask
Than simple to say
But a memory sweet
Is the hope of today

—*Jesse Cale*

ABSENCE

it's the shape of
your hands that
haunts me the
tiny crevices kept
me safe and I made
my home in
the lines that sway
in such a way that only
you could create
a safe circular
space that I seemed
to fit more
comfortably than
in my own
skin

—*Ashley Dun*

A ONE

To be a better one
To catch the wind in a sturdy sail
To selflessly hold another
To nourish my hunger

One day a better one
One day the sun will be all that fills my eyes, my lungs
The dark behind locked doors in houses from a life
long ago
My mouth will not water in the sick knots of my soul
My hands will fully extend and never fall short, out of
reach

One day
A better one

—*Jesse Cale*

LIGHT

do you remember
your first breath and
oh god
will you remember
your last?

—*Ashley Dun*

HIDDEN

maybe I see you
like a bud on a branch
bright green
young and gleaming in
the winter sun
while the branches
still scream against
the blinding snow and
maybe I see you
crawling out of the
cold ground the
first fern that
fought for life,
held out for warmth and
you have no idea how
strong your spirit is

—*Ashley Dun*

IF THIS IS LOVE

There's a run of honey behind my eyes
with feet that seem to tickle
and trickle down across the bridge of my nose
where I hold humming notes
that shake the teeth

There's a swell in the well of my heart like every
thirst could have their fill and even spill still

There's a deep lush gold rush in my arms like the breath
of a hush on my skin that's curling the tips of my lips like
a bow and a bowed cello's hello.

And at last I've forgotten the past from this rest to my
weight like my fate catching wind under wings of better
things than even memories like this kiss

If this is love I'll be above the moon by
noon and completely gone soon
So come see with me what waits above each tree,
into the sky above the sea.

—*Jesse Cale*

AFTER

nomad heart
wandering wonderful life
floating an inch off the ground
rooted nowhere and knowing
nothing of Home
this land that birthed
us doesn't even know us
doesn't want to know
just dies a slow and painful
death and this earth
this soil this air
is nothing compared
to the glittering everything that
is promised to us
the warm glow of contentment
knowing nothing of ache or want
but knowing full
and being fully known

—*Ashley Dun*

TO LOVE

To love
means
to give
to give in
to give up

To be in love
means to desire
to give
to give in
to give up

To love
is walking every mile
if it's the only way back to love

To be in love
is casting nets
until a catch in barren seas

Love
is what is takes to conquer
Life

—Jesse Cale

www.secretmidnightpress.com